CITIES OF THE WORLD

PARIS

BY R. CONRAD STEIN

CHILDREN'S PRESS®
A Division of Grolier Publishing
New York London Hong Kong Sydney
Danbury, Connecticut

CONSULTANTS

David P. Jordan, Ph.D.
Chair, Department of History
University of Illinois at Chicago

Linda Cornwell
Learning Resource Consultant
Indiana Department of Education

Project Editor: Downing Publishing Services
Design Director: Karen Kohn & Associates, Ltd.
Photo Researcher: Jan Izzo
Pronunciations: Courtesy of Tony Breed, M.A., Linguistics, University of Chicago

> ### NOTES ON FRENCH PRONUNCIATION
> *Zh* is like *s* in pleasure; *gh* is always like *g* in get. Some vowels are very much like vowels
> in English; *igh* is as in high, *ee* is as in bee, *ay* is as in day, *eh* or *e* is as *e* in bet, *ah* or *a* is as
> *a* in father, *aw* is as in draw, *oh* is as *o* in open, and *oo* is always as in boot. The sound *uh*,
> when stressed *(UH)* sounds like *u* in but; unstressed (uh), it sounds like *oo* in book, but
> much shorter and quicker. Some sounds in French do not occur in English. Notice how
> you hold your lips to say "oo," and then notice where you put your tongue to say "ee";
> now, to pronounce *ew*, hold your lips to say "oo" but move your tongue forward to say
> "ee." To say *ooh* is similar; say "ooh" as in book, but move your tongue forward to say "ay."

Library of Congress Cataloging-in-Publication Data

Stein, R. Conrad.
      Paris / by R. Conrad Stein.
         p. cm. — (Cities of the world)
      Includes index.
      Summary: Describes the history, culture, daily life, and points of
interest of the capital city of France.
      ISBN 0-516-20026-7 (lib. bdg.) — 0-516-26073-1 (pbk.)
      1. Paris (France) — Juvenile literature. [l. Paris (France)]
I. Title. II. Series: Cities of the world (New York, N.Y.)
DC707.S743   1996   96-14218
944'.361—dc20   CIP
                                                                  AC

TABLE OF CONTENTS

S E I N E

More than 100 years ago, a Boston humorist wrote this: "Good Americans, when they die, go to Paris." The man was suggesting that Paris is heaven. He was echoing a popular opinion. For generations, artists, writers, and romantic young people looked upon Paris as a heavenly place. The city inspired them with love and creativity. Life was somehow more exciting in Paris. Do Parisians think of their city in such glorious terms? Yes, most Parisians know they live in a city that is a legend around the world. Yet they also look at the everyday aspects of Paris—its streets, its shops, and especially its river.

Parisian (PEH-REE-ZHEN)

Notice the people of Paris as they walk along the River Seine. Invariably, they look at the river. Sometimes they stop, stare, and ponder its slow-moving waters. What mysteries do they see there? Perhaps they see the city's golden past. More than 2,000 years ago, a Celtic tribe called the Parisii built a settlement on one of two islands in the Seine. Over the centuries, the settlement expanded. It swelled beyond both banks of the river. Even today, many Paris streets are circular, rippling out from the island called Île de la Cité.

The Pont-Neuf and the Square du Vert Galant

These Parisians relaxing along the banks of the Seine have a wonderful view of the Île de la Cité.

Seine (SENN)
Parisii (PAH-REE-ZEE)
Île de la Cité (EEL DUH LAH SEE-TAY)

Gargoyles of
Notre Dame

Rising from the Île de la Cité is Notre Dame Cathedral (Notre-Dame de Paris). Carved on the outer walls of this haunting 700-year-old cathedral are many grotesque statues called gargoyles. The gargoyles were said to represent monsters in hell. Priests warned that sinners would be tormented by those monsters for eternity. Despite the menacing gargoyles, Parisians have always loved their cathedral.

Today, glass-topped tour boats chug slowly down the Seine, almost under the shadow of Notre Dame. Tourists come to see the city's famous attractions: the art museums, the broad avenues, and the leafy parks. Meanwhile, Parisians peer into the Seine. Its waters are their spirit.

Notre-Dame de Paris
(NOH-truh DAHM duh PAH-REE)

A Misunderstood Resident of Notre Dame

In the early 1800s, French novelist Victor Hugo wrote his classic book *The Hunchback of Notre Dame*. The story told of a man who was scorned by the people of Paris because of the hump on his back. Unwanted by his neighbors, he was forced to live in the rooftop spires of Notre Dame Cathedral. Though the man appeared hideous to most Parisians, his looks masked a gentle and kind nature. Only a few gifted people were able to see beyond his ugliness and understand his true being.

Paris is called the City of Light. Perhaps that term was born in the early 1800s, when several Paris streets were lit by gas streetlamps. Many historians believe the city earned the nickname because it is a center for the arts and a place where people fall deeply in love. Arguments over the nickname rage on and on. Visitors must decide for themselves why much of the world calls Paris the City of Light.

PARIS AND ART

Walk the streets of Paris and you will no doubt see an artist at work. The artist stands in front of an easel and busily applies brushstrokes to canvas. The Seine River is a favorite scene for painters. Later, you might see that same artist trying to sell the painting at one of the city's outdoor markets. For hundreds of years, Paris has welcomed artists.

From about 1870 to 1910, Paris hosted a revolutionary group of painters called Impressionists. Impressionists rejected the stark realism achieved by past artists.

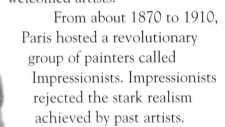

*An Édouard
Manet portrait
of artist
Claude Monet*

Many argued that the newly invented camera re-created pictures far more accurately than could any painter. Impressionist painters tried to capture colors as they changed due to the passage of light. Impressionist Claude Monet painted 40 views of one French cathedral. Each view portrayed the changing colors on the outside walls as sunlight swept over the stonework.

Claude Monet (CLOHD MOH-NAY)

Impressionists enjoyed working outdoors. Often they painted fast to capture the proper moment of light on their canvases. In Paris of the early 1900s, these artists—working quickly at their easels—were seen all over the city. They painted scenes in the parks. They painted bridges over the Seine. Often they drew crowds of onlookers who watched their pictures take form. Average Parisians became excellent art critics, as they are today.

Near the turn of the century, many foreign art students came to Paris. They were drawn by the excitement of the Impressionist movement. Vincent Van Gogh came from Holland. Van Gogh often walked out of town to paint wheat fields in the sunlight. Mary Cassatt came from Philadelphia. She painted scenes of women and children going about their everyday work and play.

Above: One of the many self-portraits painted by Vincent Van Gogh

Left: A Paris artist of today

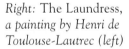

Henri de Toulouse-Lautrec
(AHN-REE DUH TOO-LOOSS
LOH-TRECK)

Right: The Laundress,
a painting by Henri de
Toulouse-Lautrec (left)

Impressionist painter Henri de Toulouse-Lautrec is revered by the people of Paris. Because of a childhood accident, his legs never grew to normal length. He thought of himself as an outcast. Toulouse-Lautrec became a citizen of the night world, frequenting the city's bars and cafes. There he painted dancing girls, entertainers, and customers. Paris high society condemned Toulouse-Lautrec's pictures as shameful.

A portrait of artist Mary
Cassatt by Edgar Degas

MASTERS OF MUSIC AND PROSE

Walk the streets of Paris and you might hear piano music drifting from an upstairs apartment. The City of Light has long been a haven for musicians and composers. In 1831, pianist Frédéric Chopin left his native Poland to live in Paris. Chopin believed that he would have greater artistic freedom in Paris. Like many artists before him, Chopin found inspiration in the City of Light. There, he wrote masterworks for the piano. In the 1920s, an African-American jazz singer named Josephine Baker went to Paris. She also sought freedom. Because she was black, Baker found few singing jobs in America at that time. But in the French capital, she was amazingly popular. Parisians loved her showmanship as well as her singing.

Ask Parisians to name their favorite singer and many will say Edith Piaf. Perhaps they will speak her name with a tear in their eye. Piaf was abandoned by her parents at a young age. She grew up singing on Paris streets to earn a few pennies. In her teens, she began a career as a nightclub performer. From nightclubs, she graduated to theaters and movies. Love ballads were Piaf's specialty.

Paris-born Edith Piaf was one of France's most well-loved singers.

Edith Piaf
(AY-DEET PYAHFF)

14

African-American jazz singer Josephine Baker found a home in Paris.

The outdoor cafes of Paris are always crowded on pleasant days.

Her husky, warm voice melted the hearts of the people of Paris. Piaf died in 1963. Her records are still heard on cafe jukeboxes. Edith Piaf remains a shining star in the City of Light.

Sit down in a Paris cafe and chat with the person next to you. Perhaps that person is a writer. Writers, too, have long flocked to the City of Light. An especially talented group of American writers came in the 1920s.

They included Ernest Hemingway, F. Scott Fitzgerald, and Gertrude Stein. All were dissatisfied with American society as it developed after World War I. Gertrude Stein called the group of American rebels the "Lost Generation." Inspired by Paris of the 1920s, the Americans wrote novels, stories, and poems that are read and studied to this day.

PARIS AND AMOUR

"I Love Paris in the Springtime." "The Last Time I Saw Paris." These are two of many songs written over the years about Paris and love. The French word for love is *amour*. Songs and poems linking Paris with amour have long delighted Parisians as well as foreigners.

No doubt the young composer Frédéric Chopin was lonely after he left Poland and settled in Paris. He met and fell in love with French novelist George Sand. Sand was a woman who used a male pen name. Few people in the early 1800s would read books written by a woman. Sand and Chopin shared moments of great happiness as well as moments of deep sorrow. They argued and they parted. Chopin died of tuberculosis at the age of thirty-nine. Some say he died of a broken heart. Theirs was a sad story. Yet millions of others who fell in love in Paris lived stories with far happier endings.

George Sand

Frédéric Chopin

amour (AH-MOOR)
Père-Lachaise (PEHR-LAH-SHEHZZ)

Without a doubt, lovers still meet in Paris and amour runs its course. On the streets, men and women walk slowly. They hold hands. When they look at each other, their faces break into smiles of pure joy. Lovers kiss in the parks. Parisians are shameless when it comes to expressing amour. The joys of love are still another reason why Paris is the City of Light.

Young love in a Paris park

A Peaceful Resting Place

Frédéric Chopin is buried in a historic cemetery—the Père-Lachaise. Designed in 1803, the cemetery is an island of greenery in the middle of a busy city. Few tourists go there. Visitors who do, walk its twisting paths and marvel at the fantastic sculptures carved into its gravestones and tombs. Other famous people buried at Père-Lachaise include Edith Piaf and Alice B. Toklas, a close friend of Gertrude Stein.

Roman general Julius Caesar commanded the Celtic village that became the city of Paris. He said of the people, "[They are] clever, inventive, and given to quarreling among themselves." Caesar made that statement about 2,000 years ago. Later history proved his observation to be correct. During the Middle Ages, from about A.D. 400 through the 1400s, scholars from all over Europe came to Paris. Many of them attended the city's university, which was founded in the twelfth century. The scholars introduced exciting ideas in art and philosophy. True to Caesar's complaint, however, the people of Paris quarreled endlessly. Eventually, their discontent exploded into the most powerful revolution ever to rock Europe.

The gardens and Palace of Versailles

LIBERTY, EQUALITY, FRATERNITY!

For hundreds of years, the kings and princes of France lived in magnificent palaces. Members of noble families stuffed themselves on lamb, beef, fish, and honey-coated desserts. Meanwhile, the common people ate only scraps of bread. Sometimes they had no bread at all. A popular story claimed that Queen Marie-Antoinette once asked an official why the people of Paris seemed to be angry all the time. "Because they have no bread," said the official. "Then let them eat cake," the queen replied. The story was probably fiction. Yet the tale was believed by impoverished Parisians who were certain their queen was cruelly indifferent to their sufferings.

Marie-Antoinette
(MAH-REE-AHN-TWAH-NET)

Then let them eat CAKE!

A painting of Queen Marie-Antoinette by Jean-Baptiste-Andre Gautier-Dagoty

Finally, the anger in Paris boiled over like a stew left too long on the fire. In the summer of 1789, bands of men and women marched through the streets. The marchers chanted the words: *"Liberté, Égalité, Fraternité!"* ("Liberty, Equality, Fraternity!"). Those words soon shook the political foundations of Europe. On July 14, 1789, thousands of Parisian commoners broke into a hated prison called the Bastille. The mob freed the prisoners held there and killed the governor of the prison. With the storming of the Bastille, the French Revolution burst over the land.

Liberté, Égalité, Fraternité! (LEE-BEHR-TAY, EE-GAH-LEE-TAY, FRAH-TEHR-NEE-TAY!)
Bastille (BAH-STEE-YUH)

The storming of the Bastille by Parisian commoners on July 14, 1789, set in motion the French Revolution.

Left: This etching by Antoine-François Sergent-Marceau shows Parisians on the streets during the night of July 13, 1789. The next day, they stormed the Bastille.

Right: This Claude Monet painting called Festivités shows a Bastille Day celebration in 1878.

Champs-Élysées (SHAHN-ZAY-LEE-ZAY)

Bastille Day

Every July 14, the people of Paris celebrate Bastille Day. The national holiday honors the capture of the despised Bastille prison in 1789. Bastille Day begins with a military parade down the Champs-Élysées, in the heart of Paris. At night, Parisians watch fireworks and dance till dawn.

The revolution ushered in the Reign of Terror. Burning with revenge, the lower classes struck back at the nobility. A beheading machine called the *guillotine* stood permanently in the center of Paris. The ruthlessly efficient machine was the brainstorm of doctor Joseph Guillotin. He said it would provide a quick, "humane" death for condemned persons. In all, some 17,000 men and women were decapitated in France during the Reign of Terror. Those who lost their heads included the king and queen, many nobles, some priests, and the defenders of those in power.

guillotine (GHEE-YOH-TEEN)

Above: A colored engraving showing the women's army marching to the Palace of Versailles in October 1789

Right: A model of the guillotine

Queen Marie-Antoinette stands at the guillotine before being executed in 1793.

Queen Marie-Antoinette met her date with the guillotine in 1793. Another woman who was beheaded scorned the revolutionaries by saying as her last words, "Ah, Liberty, what crimes are committed in thy name."

Not satisfied with merely killing their leaders, the revolutionaries also sought to destroy their buildings. Churches and palaces were hated symbols of royalty. All over France, such buildings were pulled to pieces. The despised prison known as the Bastille was torn down.

Statues of saints and kings were used for target practice by revolutionary soldiers.

A NEW PARIS

After ten years of turmoil, the violence of the French Revolution began to diminish. In 1799, army officer Napoleon Bonaparte took control of France. Napoleon led the nation into a series of wars. A brilliant military commander, he carved out a great French empire. Yet Napoleon often ruled with a harshness that recalled the kings of the past. Many French men and women believed Napoleon betrayed the revolution.

In 1852, Napoleon III, a nephew of Napoleon Bonaparte, declared himself Emperor of France. Napoleon III had grand designs to turn Paris into the most modern and elegant city on earth. To execute his plans, he turned to an administrator named Georges-Eugène Haussmann. Employing an army of workers, Haussmann tore through Paris neighborhoods that had been unchanged since the Middle Ages. With energy and stubborn determination, he created the broad boulevards that characterize Paris today.

Napoleon III and Haussmann had other reasons for their great reconstruction of the French capital. In the 1800s, small-scale revolutions continued to flare up in Paris. During the

A detail from Napoleon on Horseback, *a painting by Joseph Chabord*

Napoleon Bonaparte
(NAH-POH-LAY-AWN BAW-NAH-PART)
Georges-Eugène Haussmann
(ZHOHRZH-ew-ZHEHN ohss-MAHN)

Napoleon III (left) and Georges-Eugène Haussmann created the broad boulevards of Paris, including the Champs-Élysées.

upheavals, rebels erected barricades in the narrow, twisting streets. Fighting from the cover of those barricades, a tiny revolutionary force was able to hold off a sizable army. The wide and ruler-straight boulevards were far more difficult to barricade.

Haussmann's frenzied construction program lasted seventeen years, from 1853 to 1870. During that time, Parisian architects erected magnificent buildings along the newly created avenues. Thanks to sturdy iron beams, the buildings featured thin walls and were graced with balconies and spacious windows. Banisters and latticework decorations over doorways became a virtual adventure in metalwork. The redesign of Paris triggered a building boom that affected the city for decades to come. About half of the buildings standing in Paris today can be traced to Haussmann's seventeen-year construction marathon.

The Latin Quarter was one of the Paris neighborhoods that was rebuilt by Georges-Eugène Haussmann and Napoleon III during their seventeen-year reconstruction of Paris.

A SURVIVOR OF TWO WARS

It is September 1914, the early months of World War I. Paris is in turmoil. The German army is on the march. Advance units are only fifteen miles from Paris. Heavy guns are already lobbing shells on the French capital. Many residents pray to Ste. Geneviève. According to legend, in the year A.D. 451, the saint miraculously saved Paris from invasion by the cruel conqueror Attila the Hun. Can Ste. Geneviève deliver another miracle?

The miracle came in the form of Paris taxicabs. Answering a call from the government, the drivers of some 1,200 cabs assembled in downtown Paris. With five or six soldiers in each vehicle, the cabs raced out of town to the River Marne. There a terrible battle raged. The additional soldiers turned the tide. The "Taxicab Army" achieved a dramatic victory that is now called the "Miracle of the Marne."

Many Parisians were forced to leave the city after it fell to the Germans.

Adolf Hitler and his top aides marched in triumph down the Champs-Élysées after Paris fell to the German army in 1940.

Ste. Geneviève
  (SANT ZHEH-NEH-VYEHV)
Marne (MAHRN)
Montagne-Ste.-Geneviève
  (MAWN-TAHN-YUH-SANT-ZHEH-NEH-VYEHV)
Charles de Gaulle (SHARL DUH GOHL)

It is June 1940. World War II rages in Europe. Once more, the German army is poised outside Paris. Parisians hear artillery fire thundering from the fighting fronts. Once more, the people of Paris pray to Ste. Geneviève to save their city. This time, the saint fails to deliver a miracle. On June 12, 1940, Paris surrenders. German troops march triumphantly down the Champs Élysées, the city's major boulevard. Parisians weep at the sight.

For four years, the German army occupied the French capital. It was a time of humiliation for the French. Then, in the summer of 1944, the German army reeled backward. In Berlin, Adolf Hitler fumed over the retreat. He ordered the City of Light to be burned to the ground. The German army commander knew that Paris was the jewel of Europe, far too beautiful a city to destroy. He disobeyed Hitler's order. In late August, the bulk of the German forces pulled out, leaving the city unharmed. French leader Charles de Gaulle led a march down the Champs-Élysées. Thousands of Parisians gathered along the boulevard. They cheered and they wept tears of joy.

Saint Geneviève

Ste. Geneviève is the patron saint of Paris. A steep hill in the city center is named for her: Montagne-Ste.-Geneviève. In 1744, King Louis XV fell ill. He prayed to Ste. Geneviève and recovered. Out of gratitude, the king built a church on the top of Montagne-Ste.-Geneviève, and dedicated it to the saint. The church is now a landmark building called the Pantheon.

After the German forces left Paris in August 1944, French leader Charles de Gaulle led a victory march down the Champs-Élysées.

HOODS

The French have a saying: "The more things change, the more they stay the same." The subtle meaning behind that saying is that change takes place only on the outside of things. Paint a house, for example, and the outside coating of paint changes nothing within the house. In the last thirty years, new buildings have risen in Paris. Immigrants have arrived from foreign lands. But does this mean the city has undergone true change? Parisians think not. Their city is timeless.

TIMELESS NEIGHBORHOODS

In the United States, city families save their money and dream of moving to the suburbs. The reverse is true in Paris. New suburbs surrounding the French capital tend to be drab. The best, and certainly the most expensive, part of Paris is in the inner city. Central Paris is a small area. It's about half the size of Brooklyn, New York. It is also crowded, holding some two million people. The heart of Paris contains the theaters, the restaurants, and the sights that make Paris the City of Light.

One of the marvelous fountains at the Place de la Concorde

A sign in the Place de la Sorbonne, on the Left Bank of Paris

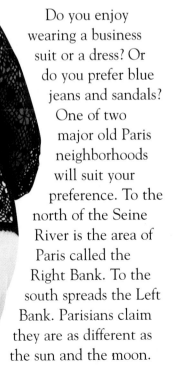

The Left Bank area of Paris is the domain of students, poets, and artists.

Sorbonne (sohr-BUHN)

Do you enjoy wearing a business suit or a dress? Or do you prefer blue jeans and sandals? One of two major old Paris neighborhoods will suit your preference. To the north of the Seine River is the area of Paris called the Right Bank. To the south spreads the Left Bank. Parisians claim they are as different as the sun and the moon.

The Right Bank is the domain of banks and office buildings. The Left Bank is home to the Sorbonne, the city's famous university. Students and poets overshadow businessmen in the Left Bank region. The distinction between the two districts began in 1253, when the Sorbonne first opened. Now, more than 700 years later, the Left Bank remains the haunt of the young. The more Paris changes, the more it stays the same.

Spreading out from the Sorbonne is a famous Left Bank neighborhood called the Latin Quarter. For centuries, the Latin Quarter was the domain of poets and philosophers. Many of those intellectuals attended the nearby Sorbonne. Even today, the Latin Quarter remains the city's intellectual center. More bookstores operate in the Latin Quarter than in any other neighborhood. In the cafes, students discuss philosophy or argue over politics.

The changes in Paris can be seen in the city's skyline. Up to the mid-1960s, few buildings in Paris were more than about eight stories high. Today, glass-and-steel high-rises pierce the sky. The new skyline leaps to the eyes of those who have not been in the city for many years. The gleaming towers are most prominent on the Right Bank.

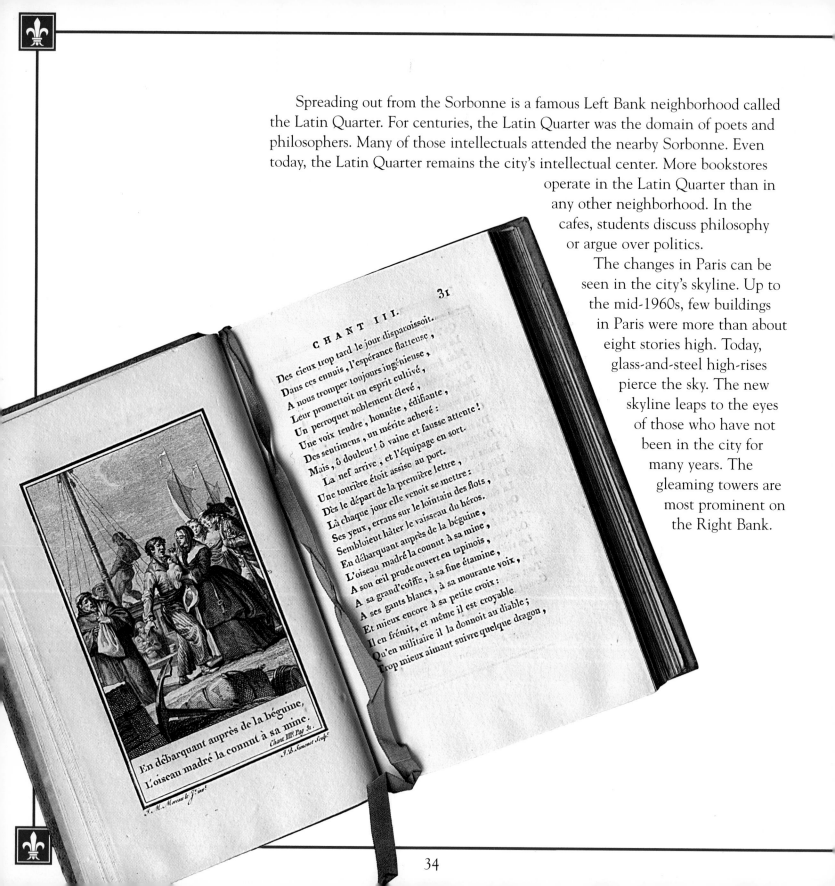

Buildings and a cafe on the Left Bank

A Paris street performer

The faces of Paris have changed, too. In the working-class suburbs live a United Nations of immigrants. They come from Algeria, the Ivory Coast, Morocco, Turkey, Tunisia, and a dozen other countries. Many of the immigrants compete for jobs with Parisians whose families have lived in the capital for generations. No one denies that tensions exist between the long-standing residents and the newcomers. Yet Paris has always welcomed immigrants. For hundreds of years, people from foreign lands have come to the French capital to establish new lives.

Parisian children with a favorite snack

The neighborhoods of Paris are connected by a remarkable subway system called the Metro. With 434 stations, the Metro covers the entire city. Rarely is one more than a few blocks from a Metro station. The system is clean, safe, and inexpensive to ride. Certainly it is popular. Metro officials report that its trains transport 1.6 billion riders a year.

Visitors often comment that Paris is remarkably clean. This is true thanks to an army of 4,500 street cleaners who descend on the avenues each morning. The cleaners used to rely solely on old-fashioned brooms

These pictures show the entrance to the Metro station at Place St. Michel (left) and the underground station itself (above).

The Hôtel de Ville (city hall) is on the Right Bank of the Seine.

Traditional Paris street cleaners still use brooms.

instead of machines to sweep up refuse. Today, modern street-cleaning machinery is also used. But there is a flaw to the city's cleanliness. The people of Paris love dogs, and there is no tradition that demands dog owners pick up after their pets. Paris folklore claims that if you step in dog leavings with your left foot you will have good luck the rest of the day. Your right foot means bad luck. Why the difference? Ask a Parisian.

GROWING UP

Notice children at play in the parks of Paris. When angry, they shout at each other: "I'll kill you!" "I'll assassinate you!" But the threats are said with a smile. The children almost never fight. Fighting in the park is simply not a French thing to do. Look at the crowded playgrounds. Children line up neatly to wait their turn at the swings and the slides. It has always been that way.

Puppeteers using hand-controlled puppets entertain children in many parks. The puppeteers are masters at their art. They make the puppets dance, wrestle, and embrace. The figures often argue in squeaky voices. Mimes also amuse children in the parks. A favorite

Marcel Marceau (MAR-SELL MAR-SOH)

The Mimes

The word *mime* is short for *pantomime*, which means "acting without words." The French have long been masters at the art of telling a story using gestures alone. Frenchman Marcel Marceau is a world-famous mime performer. Parisian mimes dress in clownlike costumes and paint their faces white. Climbing or leaning on an invisible wall is one of their most popular stunts. The mimes who perform in parks are amateurs. They hope that someone will be entertained enough to throw them a few coins.

trick for the voiceless actors is to trail inches behind a walker or a jogger, mimicking his every step.

Central Paris has one of the finest school systems in all of France. Even very wealthy parents send their children to public schools. One of the best of the city's high schools is the Lycée Janson-de-Sailly. Janson, as the young people call it, is a 110-year-old building. There, 3,200 students attend classes. Some of its teachers are published novelists. Others are well-known scientists.

Children at a Paris day-care center

Lycée Janson-de-Sailly (LEE-SAY ZHAHN-SAWN-DUH-SIGH-YEE)

PARIS AT EASE

Along the banks of the Seine you will see dozens of men and women fishing. For endless hours they sit, holding their poles, lines dangling in the water. Watch them. Almost never do they catch a fish. Still they sit, dreaming the day away. Paris is a busy, modern city. Yet it has a pace all its own.

The French term *flâner* means to stroll the streets with no particular destination in mind. Such aimless strolling is a superb way to discover the city's charms. The lucky *flâneur* might chance upon the Luxembourg Gardens. It is a classic park with gravel walkways, benches, fountains,

Feeding the pigeons in Luxembourg Gardens

An artist sketching a statue in Luxembourg Gardens

flâner (FLAH-NAY)
flâneur (FLAH-NOOHR)

People of all ages enjoy the many parks of Paris.

and an ancient wrought-iron bandstand. Some 400 years ago, the grounds were the private garden of a French queen. Today, students at the nearby Sorbonne use the Luxembourg Gardens as a hangout. Discovering surprises around every corner is one of the many delights enjoyed by the Paris *flâneur.*

Certainly a *flâneur* will stop at a sidewalk cafe to have a cool drink or some bread and cheese. Through the years, sidewalk cafes have become a signature of the French capital. Artists and writers have dreamed up masterworks while drinking coffee at a sidewalk cafe. But most people at a sidewalk cafe simply engage in the time-honored Paris pastime of people watching.

The true Parisian enjoys dining at night in one of the city's splendid restaurants. It is said that the capital's restaurant tradition dates to the time when noble families employed private chefs. Then, revolutionaries imprisoned or beheaded those families. The chefs had to look for new jobs. Thus, the great restaurants of Paris were born.

Parisians and tourists at the city's sidewalk cafes enjoy people watching while they rest and have something to drink or a bite to eat—or both.

Le Grizzli is an old-fashioned Paris bistro.

One of the most famous restaurants in the world is La Tour d'Argent, in the heart of the city. This restaurant gives diners a breathtaking view of Notre Dame Cathedral. It offers 18 varieties of duck on its menu. Its desserts are heavenly. And the prices? Don't ask. It is assumed that if you enter these places you can afford to pay the outrageous bill.

The alternative to expensive dining is to eat at one of the many bistros. A bistro is a no-frills restaurant that offers low prices and quick service. Parisians tell a story—which may be true or may be fiction—about the origin of the word bistro. After the fall of Napoleon, Russian troops briefly occupied the French capital. The soldiers must have been rude. When kept waiting in restaurants, they banged on tin plates with spoons and hollered, "bistrot," Russian for "hurry." The bistros thus became the world's first fast-food restaurants. Today, the bistros are suffering competition from McDonald's, Burger King, and their French counterpart, Quick. Young people prefer the new fast-food restaurants. Older people complain that when their favorite bistro goes out of business, a piece of the neighborhood dies with it.

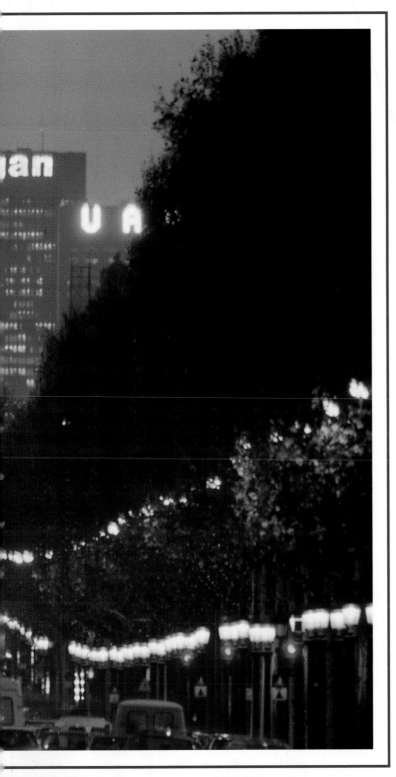

Paris is a magical destination for travelers. Some 20 million tourists visit the city each year. First-time visitors are often breathless with excitement. Anyone who has skimmed through travel books has seen thrilling pictures of Paris highlights: the Eiffel Tower, the Arc de Triomphe, Notre Dame Cathedral, the Louvre. Now the pictures spring to life. For many travelers, a tour of Paris fulfills a dream.

Eiffel (EYE-FELL)
Louvre (LOOV-RUH)
Arc de Triomphe (ARK DUH TREE-AWMF)
Notre Dame (NOH-TRUH DAHM)

THE MONUMENTS

The Eiffel Tower is the most visited and the best known of the many monuments of Paris.

What is the most visited of Paris's monuments? Without a doubt, it is the Eiffel Tower. Almost 4 million people come each year to see this famous iron structure. The tower climbs higher than a 60-story office building. To appreciate its height, stand under it, lean back, and look up. It looks like a moon rocket poised to penetrate the clouds.

The tower was designed by engineer Gustave Eiffel, who specialized in bridge building. It was completed in 1889 to celebrate the 100th anniversary of the French Revolution. When it opened, Parisians rode the cagelike elevators to the top. Many swooned at the dizzying sight of the city and countryside spreading out below them. Most architects and artists, however, despised the Eiffel Tower. They said it looked like a bridge built standing up. Some people moved out of town rather than see "that thing" from their window every morning. In 1909, the Eiffel Tower was scheduled to be demolished. It was saved only because engineers used it to hold an aerial for a newly developed radio transmitter. Today, the Eiffel Tower no longer stirs controversy. It is accepted as one of the grand symbols of Paris.

The Domed Church of Les Invalides was built during the reign of Louis XIV. The magnificent dome itself is decorated with many layers of gold leaf.

Champp-de-Mars
(SHAHN-DUH-MAHRSS)
Hôtel des Invalides
(OH-TELL DAY ZAN-VAH-LEED)

A splendid green park called the Champ-de-Mars spreads out from the Eiffel Tower. Walk the length of it, turn, and you arrive at another Paris monument: the Hôtel des Invalides (the Home for Disabled Soldiers). The residence was built out of guilt. Completed in 1676, the main building was commissioned by King Louis XIV. The king wanted a huge building to house soldiers who had been wounded in his wars. Even today, a few aging soldiers live there. Two qualities make the building famous: First, it is a marvelous example of French classical architecture; second, the building holds the tomb of Napoleon Bonaparte. Every day, hundreds of people file past the polished wooden casket where lies the army officer who conquered much of Europe.

The Arc de Triomphe is Napoleon Bonaparte's monument to his own glory. Napoleon ordered the arch to be built in 1806 to celebrate his military triumphs. It was not completed until 1836, 15 years after the general's death. The 165-foot-high arch still honors the nation's military might. France's unknown soldier is buried beneath the arch. Tourists admire the marvelous sculptures carved on its outer walls.

The Arc de Triomphe is lighted at night.

A less striking monument, from the outside at least, is Sainte-Chapelle (Holy Chapel). Erected in the 1200s, this chapel is one of the oldest buildings in Paris. From the outside, the building looks undistinguished. But a visitor entering Sainte-Chapelle is dazzled by the sunlight streaming through its stained-glass windows. The light makes the inside walls dance with colors. While walking the hall-ways, bathed with light, one has the feeling of being inside a jewel.

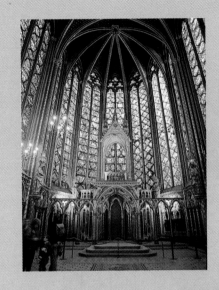

La Marsellaise, *by François Rude, is one of the sculptures that grace the Arc de Triomphe.*

Treasures of Sainte-Chapelle

King Louis IX (1214-1270) built Sainte-Chapelle for a special purpose: to display the holy relics he bought from the Emperor of Constantinople. At great expense, Louis IX purchased what the emperor claimed to be the Crown of Thorns worn by Jesus at the Crucifixion and fragments of the True Cross. For centuries, those relics were displayed within the chapel. Today, the relics are kept in Notre Dame Cathedral and are brought out only on Good Friday.

Sainte-Chapelle (SANT SHAH-PELL)

THE MUSEUM SCENE

Many experts are convinced that the Louvre is the greatest art museum in the world. So massive is its collection that to see it all would require many visits. The pride of the museum is the *Mona Lisa*, the portrait of a woman painted by Leonardo da Vinci. The mysterious smile Leonardo captured on canvas makes the *Mona Lisa* the subject of songs and poems. Another of the Louvre's treasures is the *Venus de Milo*, a magnificent Greek sculpture. The sheer perfection of the 2,000-year-old *Venus de Milo* has thrilled millions of art lovers. The Louvre has about eight miles of hallways and holds more than 30,000 paintings and sculptures. Long, slow walks through its galleries flood the senses.

The original Louvre building was a military fortress in the 1200s. Since then, it has served as a palace, a prison, and a munitions factory. Nearly every French king of importance added to the Louvre. The latest addition is a glass-and-steel pyramid that was completed in 1989. The pyramid serves as an entrance to the museum and to a vast underground shopping plaza. Because the French delight in arguing about art and

The Venus de Milo *(left) is one of the treasures of the Louvre (below).*

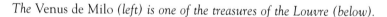

Carnavalet
(CAR-NAH-VAH-LAY)

Among the paintings in the Louvre's Grande Galerie (left) is Leonardo da Vinci's Mona Lisa.

architecture, the new pyramid has triggered a furor. Some Parisians claim it is a superb example of modern architecture. Others denounce the pyramid as a monstrosity and say it ought to be flattened.

At the Carnavalet Museum, lively displays present the history of Paris from primitive times to the present. Visitors view unique items from the city's history. Napoleon's favorite picnic basket is on exhibit. Napoleon picnicked in grand style, with 110 matching plates. Also shown is a model of the hated Bastille.

The truly ancient history of Paris comes alive underground in the Catacombs. Starting in Roman times, miners dug a beehive of tunnels under the city. The miners were looking for limestone and gypsum, materials used in making the famous plaster of Paris. As the city expanded, bodies from cemeteries were re-interred in the tunnels. Some 6 million skeletons now lie twisted in the Catacombs. Tour guides take groups on chilling visits to the mass grave sites.

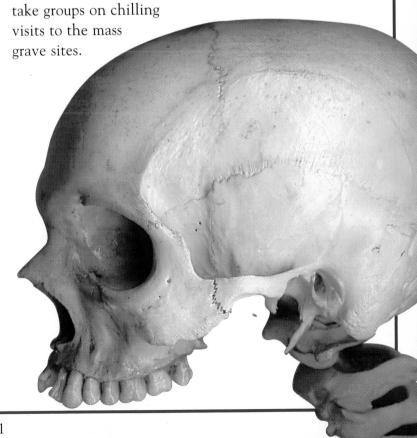

51

ALONG THE BOULEVARDS

The heartlines of Paris are its grand boulevards. Here, people gather to eat in the lively sidewalk cafes. The elegant clothing shops that make Paris the world's fashion capital stand along the boulevards. The greatest of the boulevards is the Champs-Élysées in the Right Bank neighborhood. Hundreds of years ago, a thick wall stood on the grounds of the Champs-Élysées. During the Middle Ages, the wall protected Paris from invaders. Today, the wall is gone. The Champs-Élysées is a lovely avenue lined with flower gardens and chestnut trees. Movie houses, theaters, and pricey restaurants grace the boulevard. In recent years, however, its fame has diminished its charm. Parisians complain that restaurants and shops along the Champs-Élysées try to lure foreign tourists rather than catering to city dwellers.

Boulevards lead to the city's great squares. One such square is the Place de la Concorde. Eight statues, two fountains, and a stone pillar from Egypt give the Place de la Concorde a regal look. The square was laid out in the 1740s by King Louis XV. At one time, it featured a statue of Louis XV sitting nobly atop a horse. Then the revolution broke out. The guillotine became a fixture in what is now the Place de la Concorde. Ironically, one

Cafes along the Champs-Élysées

Place de la Concorde (PLAHSS DUH LAH KAWN-KOHRD)

Montmartre (MAWN-MART-ruh)
Moulin Rouge (MOO-lan ROOZH)

The Moulin Rouge was made famous by artist Henri de Toulouse-Lautrec.

This statue of Mercury, the Greek messenger of the gods, on Pegasus, the winged horse, stands at the Place de la Concorde near an Egyptian obelisk.

of those who lost his head there was Louis XVI, the grandson of the king who first created the square.

The boulevards cut through neighborhoods that were once small towns. Such a neighborhood is Montmartre. Until the early 1800s, this hilly section was covered with wheat fields. When the Impressionist painters descended on Paris, Montmartre became a home to starving artists. Today, one of its landmarks is the Moulin Rouge (Red Windmill). It was a dance hall in 1900. Artist Henri de Toulouse-Lautrec made the Moulin Rouge famous with his vivid posters and paintings of dancing girls. The Moulin Rouge still serves as a restaurant and tavern, and Montmartre remains a neighborhood where hopeful artists gather.

The boulevards lead to bridges that span the River Seine. Thirty-five bridges cross the river as it winds an eight-mile path through the city. The Pont-Neuf dates back to 1607. Ironically, Pont-Neuf means "new bridge," even though it is the oldest bridge in the city. Some bridges are works of art and inspire lines from poets. Pont Alexandre III explodes with bronze cupids, winged horses, and other wedding-cake designs. The Pont des Arts offers walkers a magnificent view of the Île de la Cité as it parts the waters of the Seine.

Pont-Neuf (PAWN-NOOHF)
Pont Alexandre III (PAWN AH-LEG-ZAHN-DRUH TRWAH)
Pont des Arts (PAWN DAY ZAHR)

This bronze statue of Henri IV (left) stands on the Pont-Neuf (below).

Pont Alexandre III was built in 1900.

Finally, the boulevards lead to the Île de la Cité, the heart of Paris. Rising above this eternal island is Notre Dame Cathedral. The island is historic, but it is wrong to think of Paris as a museum. The city throbs with life, defying its age. Visitors soon discover why the French capital is universally hailed as the City of Light.

Many Paris monuments and bridges, including the Pont Alexandre III (right), are beautifully lit at night. Paris is literally the City of Light.

FAMOUS LANDMARKS

The Opéra

Sacré-Coeur

Notre Dame Cathedral
The cathedral on Île de la Cité is the city's most treasured church. An army of stonemasons and sculptors began working on Notre Dame in the year 1163. About 100 years later, work was completed. It is still an active church where masses are held regularly.

Sainte-Chapelle (Holy Chapel)
Also on the Île de la Cité, Sainte-Chapelle was built some 700 years ago. The chapel is an architectural masterpiece of the Middle Ages. Sainte-Chapelle's stained-glass windows flood the inside walls with dancing colors.

The Place de la Bastille
Nothing remains of the terrible prison that used to stand on this square. A tall column called the July Column rises to commemorate a July 1830 revolution against an unpopular king. In 1989, a new opera house, the Opéra de la Bastille, was completed here.

The Louvre
The world's greatest art museum now has a new glass-and-steel pyramid to serve as its front door. Parisians are divided: They either love or hate the latest addition to this ancient palace.

Sacré-Coeur
This domed basilica, one of the city's most prominent landmarks, rises from a hill above the Montmartre neighborhood.

Opéra
Completed in 1875, this spectacular opera building remains a Paris institution. In recent years, it has specialized in presenting ballets. Its stage, said to be the largest in the world, can hold 450 performers.

Eiffel Tower

La Madeleine

Arc de Triomphe

La Madeleine
A church built like a Greek temple, La Madeleine is a prime site for society weddings and funerals of important men and women. People whose funeral masses have been held there include Frédéric Chopin and jazz singer Josephine Baker.

Arc de Triomphe
Built to celebrate the many triumphs of Napoleon's army, the arch is a symbol of Paris.

St.-Étienne-du-Mont
Because this church was built over a 150-year span, it blends different architectural styles. Finally completed in 1626, its organ is covered with fantastic designs.

Sorbonne
This university is the headquarters of the Left Bank youth culture.

Palais du Luxembourg
Rising over the Luxembourg Gardens, this one-time palace has an Italian design. It was built by Marie de' Médici in the 1600s. Today, the French senate meets here.

Eglise de St.-Sulpice
Often called the "Cathedral of the Left Bank," the inside walls of St.-Sulpice are graced with magnificent murals.

Hôtel des Invalides
A military museum and the tomb of Napoleon are found in this building, which was originally constructed to house disabled soldiers.

Eiffel Tower
The tower is the most visited monument in all Paris. Tourists must wait in long lines to take the elevator to the top, but the spectacular view is worth the wait.

FAST FACTS

POPULATION   1990
City: 2,175,200
Metropolitan Area: 9,060,257

AREA
City: 41 sq. miles
Metropolitan Area: 185 sq. miles

NEIGHBORHOODS   The city's oldest neighborhood surrounds the Île de la Cité and the Île St.-Louis, two islands in the Seine River. Over the centuries, the city expanded from the Île de la Cité. Therefore, some streets and subway routes are circular. The famous and historic sites of Paris lie within a 22-mile ring-shaped road called the Boulevard Périphérique. The suburbs beyond the Périphérique are less distinguished and attract few tourists. Two major neighborhoods are prominent in historic Paris. The Right Bank, north of the River Seine, is a section devoted to banks, offices, and corporation headquarters. The Left Bank, south of the river, is home to the Sorbonne and a student culture. Other neighborhoods, such as Montmartre and Montparnasse, were once separate towns. Though they are now part of historic Paris, they retain a small-town identity.

CLIMATE   Rain and chilly weather prevail in the winter and in the spring. The fall climate is ideal, with September and October the best months. The city's average January temperature is 28 degrees Fahrenheit; the average July temperature is 68 degrees Fahrenheit.

INDUSTRIES   Paris is the capital of France, and many of its residents hold government jobs. The city and its suburbs also produce the majority of the automobiles made in France. The capital is a center for book publishing and the manufacture of furniture, electronic equipment, chemicals, and dyes. Paris is the nation's transportation hub—a meeting place for highways and railroad lines. Three major airlines serve the French capital. The Paris subway (the Metro) has more than 100 miles of track. Paris sets the style for world fashions. Small shops in the heart of the city produce elegant women's clothing for expensive stores throughout the world. Other luxury items made in the city include jewelry and perfume.

CHRONOLOGY

About 300 B.C.
A Celtic tribe called the Parisii begins a settlement on the Île de la Cité.

53 B.C.
Roman troops under Julius Caesar occupy the island settlement.

A.D. 451
Ste. Geneviève is credited with saving the city from conqueror Attila the Hun.

1163
Construction begins on Notre Dame Cathedral.

1253
Robert de Sorbon founds Sorbonne College in Paris.

1348
The Great Plague (Black Death) strikes Paris.

1364-1383
King Charles V builds many new buildings, including the Bastille.

1643
Louis XIV, the Sun King, becomes king of France.

1789
The French Revolution begins; mobs storm the Bastille.

1793-1794
During the Reign of Terror, revolutionaries behead hundreds of nobles and counterrevolutionaries.

1804
Napoleon proclaims himself Emperor of France.

1853-1870
Napoleon III and Georges-Eugène Haussmann undertake the radical reconstruction of Paris.

Notre Dame Cathedral

1889
The Eiffel Tower is completed.

1914
The "Taxicab Army" saves Paris from an attack by the German army.

1940
Paris surrenders to German forces in World War II.

1944
Paris is liberated; General Charles de Gaulle leads a triumphant march down the Champs-Élysées.

1973
The 58-story Maine-Montparnasse Tower, the tallest building in France, is completed; after the building's completion, laws limited the height of future high-rises in the French capital.

1974
Les Halles, a food market that served Parisians for hundreds of years, is removed; engineers determine that Les Halles has become a traffic hazard; many Parisians are saddened to see the old market destroyed.

1989
A pyramid-shaped entrance is added to the Louvre; many Parisians dislike the structure.

1992
The theme park Euro Disney opens in the Paris suburb of Marne-la-Vallée.

1995
Two terrorist bombs rip through the Paris Metro, killing seven passengers and injuring 150 others.

PARIS

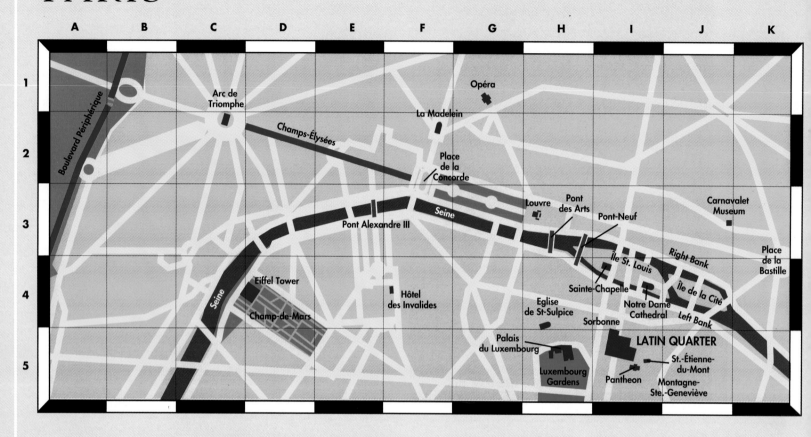

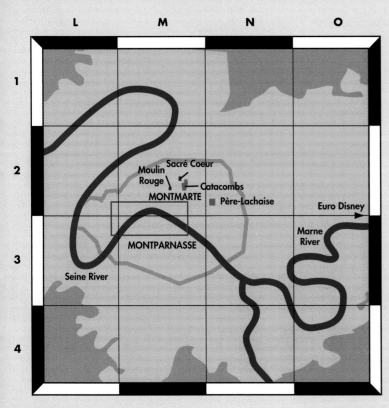

The red rectangle on this map is the area shown on the page 60 map.

GLOSSARY

fraternity: Brotherhood

frenzied: Hectic or hurried

frill: An unnecessary addition to a service; a luxury

furor: A state of great excitement

gargoyle: An ugly carving that was meant to inspire the fear of hell

haven: A safe place; a place of refuge

inspiration: An influence that helps someone do especially good work

ironically: Showing a startling difference between what might be expected and what actually occurred

peer: To stare at intently

ponder: To think deeply

regal: Kingly

subtle: Apparent but not obvious

swoon: To faint

turmoil: Extreme confusion

Picture Identifications

Cover: Bronze statue at the Palais de Chaillot; the Arc de Triomphe; the flag of France; French schoolchildren
Title page: Buying a treat for a child at the Luxembourg Gardens
Pages 4-5: A boat cruise along the Seine River
Pages 8-9: The École Militaire as seen from the base of the Eiffel Tower
Pages 18-19: *The Storming of the Bastille*, a painting by Jean-Baptiste Lallemand showing the people arming themselves at the Hôtel des Invalides
Pages 30-31: A protest parade on the streets of Paris
Pages 44-45: The Champs-Élysées and the Arc de Triomphe at sunset

Photo Credits:

Cover (top left), ©M. Howell/**N E Stock Photo;** cover (background), ©Brent Winebrenner/**mga/Photri;** cover (top right), ©**KK&A, Ltd.;** cover (right), ©David Frazier/**Folio, Inc.;** 1, ©Naomi Duguid/**Asia Access;** 3, ©**KK&A, Ltd.;** 4-5, ©**Robert Fried;** 6 (top), ©Reparant/Slide/**Photo Edit;** 6 (bottom), ©Koechlin/Slide/**Photo Edit;** 7 (left), ©Michael Carroll/**N E Stock Photo;** 7 (right), **Springer/Corbis-Bettmann;** 8-9, ©Geraldine LiaBraaten/**Bonnie Kamin;** 9, The Art Journal/**Mary Evans Picture Library;** 10 (left), ©Bruce Leighty/**mga/Photri;** 10-11 (palette), ©**KK&A, Ltd.;** 11, **Planet Art,** *The Impressionists* **CD ROM;** 12 (left), ©Bachmann/ **N E Stock Photo;** 12 (right), Musée d'Orsay/**Art Resource, NY;** 13 (top right), **Planet Art,** *The Impressionists* **CD Rom;** 13 (bottom right), **National Portrait Gallery, Smithsonian Institution/Art Resource, NY;** 13 (left), **Mary Evans Picture Library;** 14, **Archive/Imapress;** 15 (left), ©Popperfoto/**Archive Photos;** 15 (right), ©M. Hahn/Slide/**Photo Edit;** 16 (heart), ©**KK&A, Ltd,** 16 (left), **Mary Evans Picture Library;** 16 (right), ©Hackett/**Archive Photos;** 17 (top), ©**Robert Fried;** 17 (bottom), ©Petri/Slide/ **Photo Edit;** 18-19, Musée Carnavalet/**AKG Photo, London;** 20 (top), ©**Robert Fried;** 20 (French bread), ©**KK&A, Ltd.;** 21(French pastry), ©**KK&A, Ltd;** 21 (bottom), **AKG Photo, London;** 22, Palais de Versailles, Musée Historique/**AKG Photo, London;** 23 (top left), **AKG Photo, London;** 23 (top right), **Planet Art,** *The Impressionists* **CD ROM;** 23 (French flag), ©**KK&A, Ltd.; 24** (both pictures), Musée Carnavalet/ **Giraudon/Art Resource;** 25, **Mary Evans/Explorer;** 26, Museo Napoleonico/**Art Resource, NY;** 27 (top), **AKG Photo, London;** 27 (bottom), **Mary Evans Picture Library;** 28(left), **Archive Photos/Potter Collection;** 28 (right), **Archive Photos;** 29 (left), **Archive Photos;** 29 (right), ©J. Nettis/**H. Armstrong Roberts;** 30-31, ©**Robert Fried;** 32 (top), ©Michael J. Pettypool/**Dave G. Houser;** 32 (bottom), ©**Robert Fried;** 33 (both pictures), ©**Robert Fried;** 34, ©**KK&A, Ltd;** 35 (top left), ©J. Nettis/**H. Armstrong Roberts;** 35 (top right), ©Naomi Duguid/**Asia Access;** 35 (bottom), ©**Ben Klaffke;** 36 (both pictures), ©**Robert Fried;** 37 (left), ©Michael Carroll/**N E Stock Photo;** 37 (right), ©Naomi Duguid/**Asia Access;** 38 (left), **Archive Photos/Express Newspapers;** 38 (marionette), ©**KK&A, Ltd.;** 39 (left), ©**Robert Fried;** 39 (court jester hand puppet), ©**KK&A, Ltd.;** 40 (left), ©**Robert Fried;** 40 (right), ©Larime Photographics/**Dembinsky Photo Assoc.;** 41 (top), ©**Photri, Inc.;** 41 (bottom), ©**Cameramann International, Ltd.;** 42 (bottom), ©Jan Butchofsky-Houser/**Dave G. Houser;** 42-43 (baguette and cheese), ©**KK&A, Ltd.;** 43, ©Jan Butchofsky-Houser/**Dave G. Houser;** 44-45, ©Petri/Slide/**Photo Edit;** 46, ©R. Kord/**H. Armstrong Roberts;** 47 (top), ©**Robert Fried;** 47 (bottom right), ©**KK&A, Ltd.;** 48, ©Slide/**Photo Edit;** 49 (left), ©C. Ursillo/**H. Armstrong Roberts;** 49 (right), ©Slide/**Photo Edit;** 50 (left), ©Michael J. Pettypool/**Dave G. Houser;** 50 (right), ©**Robert Fried;** 51 (top), ©**Robert Fried;** 51 (skull), ©**KK&A, Ltd.;** 52, ©Bachmann/**N E Stock Photo;** 53 (top), ©**Robert Fried;** 53 (bottom), ©Philip H. Coblentz/**Dave G. Houser;** 54 (left), ©**Robert Fried;** 54-55, ©Ansara/Slide/**Photo Edit;** 55 (top), ©Slide/**Photo Edit;** 55 (bottom right), ©Petri/Slide/**Photo Edit;** 56 (left), ©Marin/Slide/**Photo Edit;** 56 (right), ©Greg Gawlowski/ **Dembinsky Photo Assoc.;** 57 (left), ©Larime Photographics/**Dembinsky Photo Assoc.;** 57 (middle), ©Bachmann/**N E Stock Photo;** 57 (right), ©Gianina/Slide/**Photo Edit;** 59, ©R. Kord/**H. Armstrong Roberts;** 60 & 61, ©**KK&A, Ltd.**

INDEX

Page numbers in boldface type indicate illustrations

ABOUT THE AUTHOR

R. Conrad Stein was born and grew up in Chicago. After serving in the Marine Corps, he attended the University of Illinois, where he earned a degree in history. He later studied in Mexico. He is the author of numerous books written for young readers. Mr. Stein lives in Chicago with his wife and their daughter Janna. The author has traveled much of the world, and he considers Paris to be one of the most beautiful cities he has ever seen.